Top of Europe

Switzerland Alps via Cogwheel Railway

Jane Moorman

Introduction

The desire to reach the top of mountains seems to be a a part of the exploration drive in humans. Many people trek to the top of the mountains no matter if they are under 10,000 feet elevation or Mt Everest at 29,031 feet.

The Alps of Europe have challenged mountaineers since the 1800s. As the men conquered the mountains to reach the summits, their tales of the trek influenced others to challenge themselves to the task.

Even women got involved in mountaineering. British mountaineer Lucy Walker was the first woman to regularly climb in the Alps, including reaching the Matterhorn summit in 1871. As the pioneer of women climbers, she completed a total of 98 expeditions.

Royalty has also been attracted to the mountains. Queen Victoria visited Lucerne, Switzerland, in 1868 for a break from monarch duties. During her five-week stay, she rode to the top of Mount Pilatus on her pony, Flora. The trek lasted four days, including three nights at Furka Pass.

With the invention of steam-powered trains, man's desire to conquer mountains drove them to forge railways to the top of mountains.

Using the technology of rack, or cog, railways and tunneling, they were able to provide ways for non-mountaineers to experience breathtaking views of the Alps from above.

Rack railways, also called rack-and-pinion, cog or cogwheel, is a steep grade railway. The trains are fitted with one or more cog wheels or pinions that mesh with a rack rail.

This allows the trains to operate on steep grades above 10 percent, which is the maximum for friction-based rail.

The first mountain cog railway was opened in 1868 on Mount Washington in New Hampshire. The first mountain rack railway in continental Europe was opened in 1871 on Mount Rigi in Switzerland.

Three popular European cog railway destinations are Mount Pilatus, Jungfraujoch and Gornergrat to view the Matterhorn. Pilatus railway opened in 1889, while the Gornergrat railway was completed in 1898, and Jungfraujoch was finished in 1912.

During the summer of 2022, I traveled on these alpine railways to view the Switzerland Alps. This book shares my experience with you.

Enjoy!

Jane Moorman, photographer

Lucerne, Switzerland
Gateway to Mount Pilatus

Church of St. Leodegar, built in 1633, is one of Lucerne's landmarks. The towers are surviving remnants of the original church built in 735.

Lake Lucerne

Lake Lucerne with Mt. Pilatus in the background. The lake fills the Reuss River valley for a total area of 44 square miles at an elevation of 1,424 feet, with a maximum depth of 702 feet. Much of the shoreline rises steeply into mountains, resulting in many picturesque views, including those of the mountains Pilatus and Rigi.

The "Golden Round Trip" — a favorite among tourists — involves taking a boat from Lucerne across Lake Lucerne to Alpnachstad. From there, visitors go up on the cogwheel railway, coming down on the aerial cableways and panorama gondolas, and taking a bus back to Lucerne.

Pilatus Railway

The world's steepest cog-wheel railway connects Alpnachstad with Mt. Pilatus summit, with a maximum gradient of 48 percent and an average gradient of 35 percent.

Eduard Locher, an engineer with great practical experience, proposed the rail system.

The design placed a horizontal double rack between the two rails with the rack teeth facing each side to prevent the car from jumping out of engagement at the greater gradient.

Construction began in March 1886. It took three summers for 600 laborers to complete the rail system. The line opened on June 4, 1889. It was electrified in 1937, using an overhead electric supply of 1,650 volts.

The government provided no financial help for the construction; instead, Locher established his own company, "Locher Systems," to build the 2.86-mile railway.

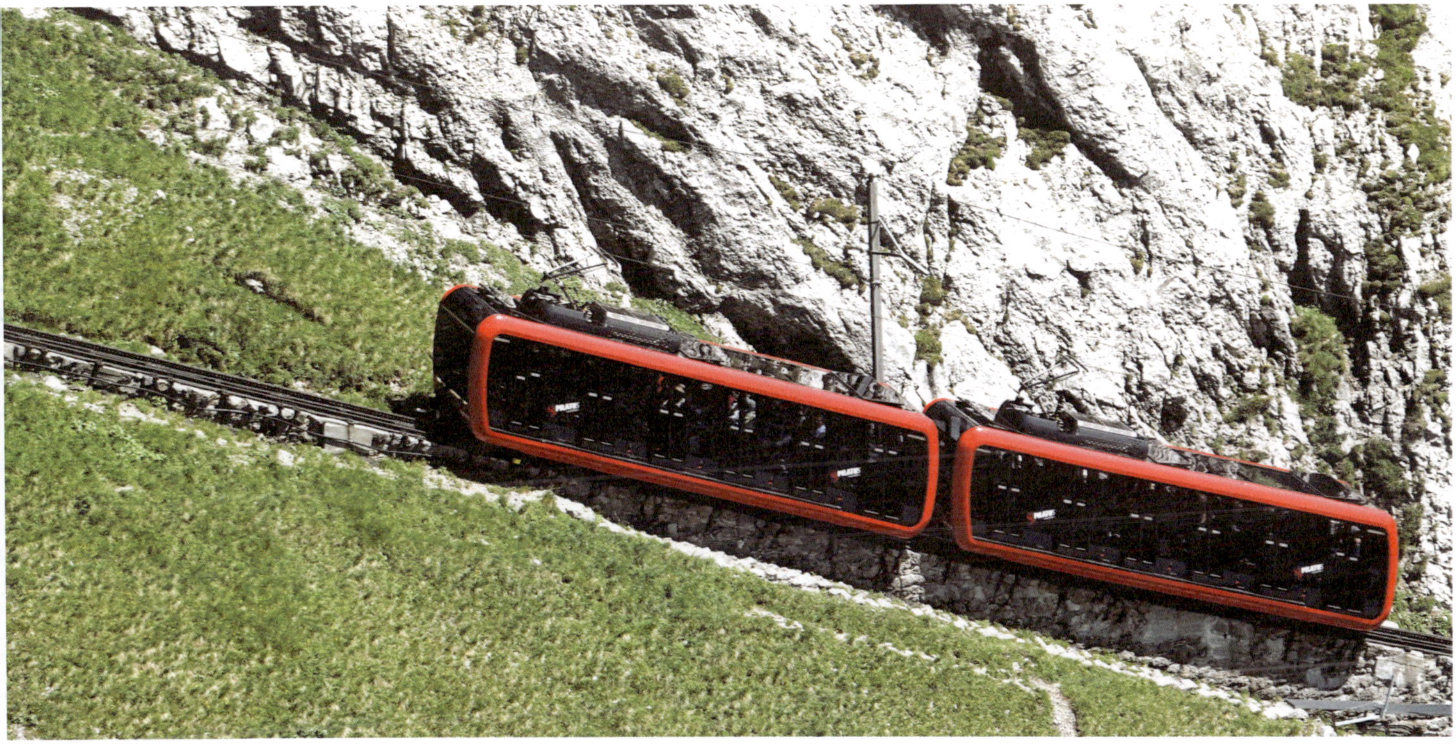

PILATUS
LUZERN
43

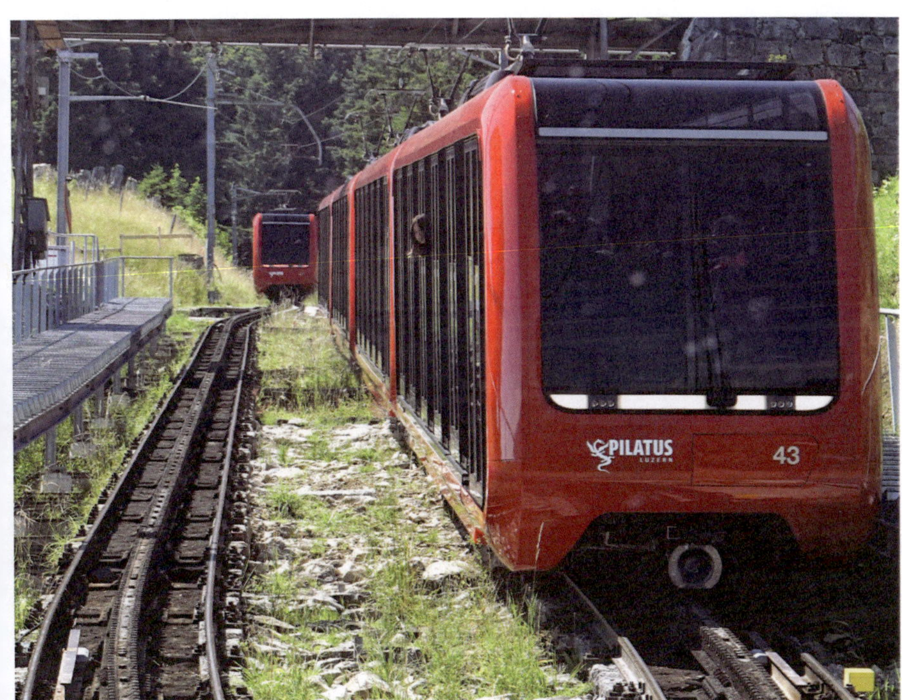

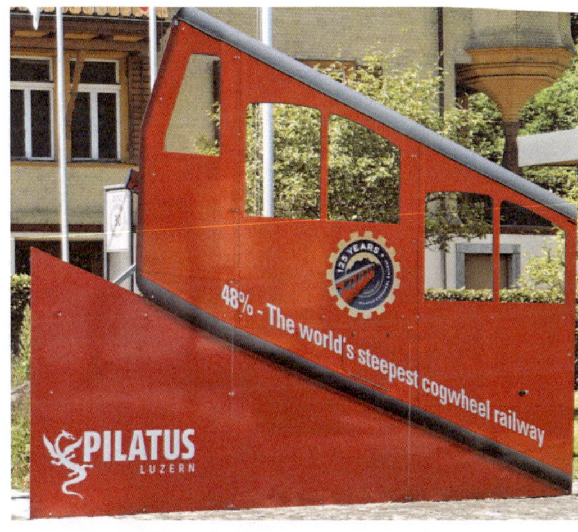

48% - The world's steepest cogwheel railway
PILATUS
LUZERN

Pilatus-Kulm

Pilatus Kulm, the mountain's summit, is nearly 7,000 feet above sea level. Peaks include Tomlishorn (6,983 feet), Esel (6,949 feet), and Oberhaupt (6,906 feet).

There are several legends regarding the origin of the mountain's name. One claims it was named because Pontius Pilate was buried there— not.

Another is that the mountain looks like the belly of a large man, Pilate, lying on his back. The name may also be derived from "pileatus," meaning cloud-topped.

There are many legends and myths surrounding Mount Pilatus. In the Middle Ages, people believed that healing dragons lived in the bare caves of Mount Pilatus.

There are two hotels, Hotel Pilatus-Kulm and Hotel Bellevue, and six restaurants in the summit facility where the Pilatus Railway and the gondola bring visitors to enjoy the astonishing view and hike the many trails.

Dragon Way, Oberhaupt Trails

The Dragon Way trail circum-navigates the Tonlishorn Oberhaupt peaks.

View
From
Mount
Pilatus
of
the
Swiss
Alps

Kilmsenhorn Chapel on Mount Pilatus
View of Klimsenhorn from the Dragon Way trail.

The Hergiswil entrepreneur Kaspar Blattler built the Hotel Klimsenhorn on the Klimsenhorjoch in the Pilatus massif at 6,115 feet (1854 meters) above sea level from 1856-1860. The complex also included an architecturally independent Neo-Gothic chapel, which was inaugurated in 1861.

After the closure and demolition of the hotel in 1967, the chapel building remained, but was only used as a shelter for climbers.

In 1974 a Swiss named Alois Hediger got involved to preserve the chapel. The restoration was completed after one year. Consecration took place on Sept. 7, 1975.

Klimsen Chapel is located on the 6.3 km trail that circles Klimsenhorn, which is a beautiful pre-peak of Mount Pilatus that lies a few meters above the chapel.

The chapel can be seen from the Dragon Way trail, above photo, and with binoculars from Lake Lucerne.

The Foundation Chapel Klimsenhorn is dedicated to the preservation of the chapel. Since 2002, the Klimsen Chapel is under monument protection.

North Side of Mount Pilatus

View of the 'backside' of Mount Pilatus from the gondola.

The descent from the summit of Pilatus-Kulm via the aerial cableway is called the "Dragon Ride." This gondola holds about 20 people. The gondola has top-to-bottom windows for amazing views that give a sensation of flying.

In less than four minutes, the riders reach the little hamlet of Frankmuntegg.

People transfer to a cable car for a 30-minute ride through Krienseregg to the small hamlet of Kriens.

Sights from the Cable Car

End of the Ride

At the terminal in Kriens is a statue of a dragon made from recycled metal tools.

Interlaken, Switzerland
Gateway to Jungfraujoch, Top of Europe

Route to Jungfraujoch

The unique round-trip takes you from Interlaken by bus to Grindelwald, followed by the modern Wengernalpbahn cogwheel railway first to Kleine Scheidegg, which sits at an altitude of 2,061m at the foot of the notorious Eiger North Wall.

From here, the Jungfrau Railway travels through the Eiger tunnel to the stations at Eigerwand and Eismeer, with a five-minute stop at each to allow passengers to enjoy spectacular sightseeing through large observation windows hewn from solid Alpine Rock.

Finally, the arrival on the Jungfraujoch, in the heart of a glorious glacier world on the very roof of Europe!

Return to Grindelwald via gondolas for clear views of the mountain valley.

Jungfraujoch

The Jungfraujoch, German literally "maiden saddle," is a glacier saddle connecting two major 4000ers of the Bernese Alps: the Jungfrau and the Monch. It is at an elevation of 11,362 feet. (3,463 m).

It is overlooked by the rocky prominence of the Sphinx.

Wengernalpbahn

Wengernalpbahn is the world's longest continuous cogwheel railway at 11.87 miles from Lauterbrunnen to Grindelwald vias Wengen and Kleine Scheidegg. The name refers to the alpine meadow of Wengernalp above Wengen.

Most passengers transfer at Keline Scheidegg to the Jungfrau Railway to continue their journey to the highest railway station in Europe at Jungfraujoch.

Jungfraubahn

Jungfruabahn, or Jungfrua Railway, is the highest cogwheel railway in Europe. It runs from Kleine Scheidegg to the Jungfruajoch railway station is at 11,320 feet above sea level.

Adolf Guyer-Zeller first though of the idea to build a tunnel to the mountain top in 1893. Building began in 1896 and took 16 years to complete.

Upon leaving Kleine Scheidegg the railway enters the 4.3 mile long tunnel with a gradient of up to 25 percent.

Along the way there is a station with windows to view the mountain view. The windows are placed in holes used to remove excavated rocks from the tune during construction.

Sphinx Observatory on Jungfraujoch

Perched precariously above the Jungfraujoch railway sits the Sphinx Observatory, a scientific observation and research facility. It gained its name after the rocky summit on which it is located.

This high-altitude observatory is one of the world's highest observatories at 11,782 feet (3,571m) and the second-highest observation deck in Switzerland.

The observation deck is accessible to the public through a tunnel fitted with an elevator that ascends to the observatory from the Jungfrau railway station.

The open viewing deck offers views of the Jungfrau, Monch and Eiger peaks, all within a few miles.

Monch Peak

From the Sphinx Observatory observation deck, the Monch, German literally "monk," mountain is the closest peak. The Monch forms part of a mountain ridge between the Jungfrau and Jungfraujoch to the west and the Eiger to the east.

The Jungfrau railway tunnel runs right under the summit at an elevation of approximately 10,830 feet (3,300m).

The Great Aletsch Glacier

At 14 miles (22km), the Aletsch Glacier is the longest ice stream in the Alps. Beginning on the Jungfraujoch, it is composed of four smaller glaciers converging at Konkordiaplatz. The whole area, including other glaciers, is part of the Jungfrau-Aletsch Protection Area, which was declared a UNESCO World Heritage Site in 2001.

Visitors to the mountain top may venture out on the solid ice and snow of the Great Aletsch Glacier and get a bird's eye view of the glacier on a zipline flight. Other activities include sledding on the glacier.

Ice Palace

There are many attractions on the Jungfraujoch, including the glistening Ice Palace, where visitors walk through an ice tunnel to view various sculptures created out of ice.

Penguins and polar bears are among the sculptures, including one honoring Chinese pianist Lang Lang, who performed live outdoors at the Top of Europe.

Other attractions include the Ice Gateway, a 360-degree cinematic experience, the High Alpine Research Exhibition, and opportunities for hiking on and through the glacier. Visitors can also enjoy the highest Lindt chocolate shop and several restaurants.

Ice sculpture of Chinese pianist Lang Lang

Ice sculpture of igloo with penguins.

Return to Grindelwald

From snow and ice glaciers to green valleys. Return to Grindelwald via gondolas for clear views of the mountain valley.

One final view of the Top of Europe from the descending gondola.

Zermatt, Switzerland
Gateway to Gornergrat and the Matterhorn

Route to Gornergrat

Zermatt, Switzerland, is the starting point of the Gornergrat Cog railway.

End of the Ride

The Gornergrat Bahn is the highest open-air railway in Europe. It travels 5.8 miles (9.34 km) from Zermatt to the Gornergrat, with an altitude difference of 4,820 feet.

The line opened in 1898 and was the first electric cog railway built in Switzerland and the highest until the Jungfrau Railway was built in 1912.

It travels through Riffelalp and Riffelberg stations, where passengers may connect with trails for hiking and visit restaurants and hotels.

    Upon disembarking at the Gornergrat station, visitors discover the Kulmhotel Gornergrat and restaurant, a chapel, and Zooom: The Matterhorn —a captivating interactive exhibit including a 3D cinema and virtual paragliding flights with 3D glasses while in a specially designed floating armchair.

    Because of the good climatic conditions at the altitude of 10,285 feet, astronomical observatories have been located in both towers of the Kulnhotel Gornergrat since 1967. The Gornergrat Infrared Telescope was located in the north tower observatory until decommissioned in March 2005.

    The project "Stellaurium Gornergrat: is located in the south tower observatory.

    The highlight of the Gornergrat is the observation deck that provides a 360-degree view of the mountains.

Gornergrat

Gornergrat, Gorner Ridge in English, is a rocky ridge of the Pennine Alps, 10,200 feet (3100 m) above sea level, overlooking the Gorner Glacier.

The summit of Gornergrat offers a view of 28 4000-meter peaks, whose highest are Duforspitz at 15,203 feet (4634 m), Dom at 14,915 feet (4546 m), Liskamm at 14,852 feet (4527 m), Weisshorn at 14,780 feet (4505 m), and Matterhorn at 14,691 feet (4478 m).

The Gorner Glacier, German: Gornergletscher, formed by numerous smaller glaciers, flows through an area viewed from the Gronergrat.

Dufourspitze is tallest in the Gornergrat at 15,203 feet (4634 m).

Matterhorn glacier begins at Klein Matterhorn (Little Matterhorn) the peak

The Matterhorn

Matterhorn has a near-symmetric pyramid peak, with four steep faces facing the four compass points.
It remained unclimbed after most of the other great Alpine peaks had been attained. The first ascent of
the Matterhorn was in 1865 by a party led by Edward Whymper.
The north face was not climbed until 1931. The west face, the highest of the four sides, was completely
climbed only in 1962.

![Gorner Glacier panorama]

Gorner Glacier on left, Grenzgletscher on right, framing the Monte Rosa massif.

Gorner Glacier

The Gorner Glacier is about 7.7 miles long and slightly less than a mile wide. The entire glacial area is 20 square miles, which makes it the second-largest glacier system in the Alps after the Aletsch Glacier system. However, in length, it ranks third behind the Aletsch and Fiescher glaciers.

A notable feature of this glacier is the Gornersee, an ice marginal lake at the confluence area of the Gorner Glacier and Grenzgletscher. (Seagreen circle in photo) This lake fills every year and drains in summer, usually as a glacial lake outburst flood. This is one of only a few glacial lakes in the Alps exhibiting this behavior.

A small waterfall, right photo, forms when the glacial lake outbursts causing a flood.

Grenzgletscher

Grenzgletscher, English meaning Border Glacier, between the central Monte Rosa massif and the Liskamm to the south, is the main contributor to the lower Gorner Glacier.

Retreating Gorner Glacier

Like almost all other glaciers in the Alps, the Gomer Glacier is retreating as a result of global warming. As of 2014 it had been retreating about 98 feet every year. In 2008, there was a record loss of 950 feet.

As of about 2015, the Goner Glacier had retreated to the point where it lost touch with its main tributary: the Grenzletscher on the south side of the Monte Rose massif. Now, the prominent flow visible from Gornergrat is officially called Grenzgletscher and can no longer be considered part of the Gorner Glacier. The Monte Rosa Glacier has also lost touch with the Gorner Glacier.

About the Photographer

Jane Moorman describes herself as an adventurer who loves to drive the backroads to see what there is to see.

During her 30-year journalism career, Jane honed her photographic skills as a photojournalist, including covering high school sporting events.

A friend once said, "I wish I could see the world as Jane sees it. Finding the beauty in things that most of us don't take time to see."

Upon retiring in 2021, Jane decided there was a lot of the world she had not visited, so she began her journey of exploring the world.

In 2023, Jane visited two places on her bucket list — Switzerland to see the Alps and Kenya for an African Safari.

She currently lives in Albuquerque, New Mexico, but says her real home is on the road.

When she is not on the road, she is at home building

photo books of her various adventures.

She currently has published books on the Great Lake Lighthouses, several United States state capitol buildings, as well as other interesting things she has discovered during her travels.

Her books are available on Amazon.com and other digital book platforms.

www.ingramcontent.com/pod-product-compliance
Lightning Source LLC
Chambersburg PA
CBRC100834110726
48006CB00009B/1389